To:

Alexis James

From:

Released Time Christian Education

Date:

December 11, 2013

The Prayer That Makes God Smile

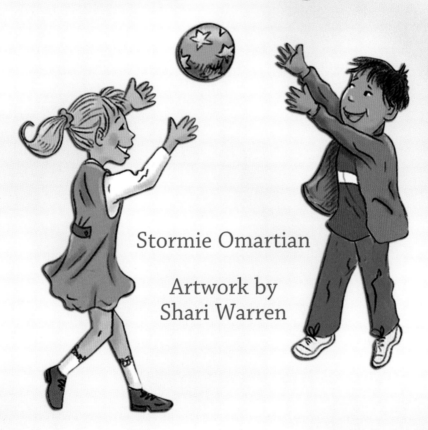

Stormie Omartian

Artwork by
Shari Warren

HARVEST HOUSE PUBLISHERS
EUGENE, OREGON

The Prayer That Makes God Smile

Text Copyright © 2009 by Stormie Omartian
Art Copyright © 2009 by Shari Warren. Licensed by Bentley Licensing Group.

Published by Harvest House Publishers
Eugene, Oregon 97402
www.harvesthousepublishers.com

ISBN 978-0-7369-2314-9
ISBN 978-0-7369-5892-9 (The 1687 Foundation Edition)

Back cover photo © Michael Gomez Photography

Design and production by Mary pat Design, Westport, Connecticut

13 14 15 /QG/ 12 11 10 9 8 7 6 5 4 3 2 1

The 1687 Foundation First Printing, 2013

Printed in the United States of America

It's never too soon to lead a child to Jesus.
—STORMIE OMARTIAN

Jesus said, "Let the little children come to Me and do not forbid them."
—MATTHEW 19:14

You make God happy. That's because He loves you. God loves all little boys and girls. **He loves you** when you **do good things,** like helping others. But He also loves you even when you do things that are not so good, like forgetting to put away your toys.

God loves you when you are **happy,** and He loves you when you are **sad.** God loves you when you are **sleeping,** and He loves you when you are **awake.** There is never a time when God does not love you.

"Thank You, God, for loving me all the time."

God shows His love for you by giving you good food to eat, clean water to drink, and a warm, cozy place to live. He also shows His love by giving you the rain and the sun, the flowers and the trees, and adorable animals like puppies and kittens to enjoy.

One of the most wonderful ways God shows His love for you is by giving you a family. Some families are big and some are small. Your family might have ten people in it, or it might just be a family of two. Yet every family is a gift from God. When we thank God for our families—and for all the gifts He gives us—it makes Him happy.

"Thank You, God, for my family, and for all the other gifts You give to me."

Another way God shows His love for you is by giving you His Word to read. When you read the Bible, it makes God happy. That's because the Bible teaches you how to know and obey God and how to do what is right.

God gives us rules to live by because He loves us and doesn't want us to get hurt. When you obey God's rules and do what is right, God is happy.

"Thank You, God,
for giving me the Bible
to read. Help me
to obey Your rules."

God loves you so much that He **always** listens to you when you talk to Him. Talking to God is called praying. He loves it when you talk to Him. Your prayers make God happy.

God always wants you to ask Him for the things you **need.** He already knows what you need, but He still wants You to talk to Him about it. That's because He loves you and wants you to spend time with Him. God is happy when you ask Him for the things you need.

God also wants you to **ask Him** for the things you **want.** There is a difference between the things you **want** and the things you **need.**

The **things you need** are what you **must have** in order to live—like a home, clothes to wear, or something to take when you are sick that **will help you** get well.

The **things you want** are things you don't have to have in order to live, but you **want them anyway**—like a bicycle to ride, a fun game, or a new friend to play ball with.

God always gives us what we need.
But He doesn't always give us what we
want. That's because God knows
what is best for us. He gets to decide
if He will give us what we want or not.
And He decides when to give it to us.
We can trust Him to do the right
thing for us because He loves us so
much.

"Thank You, God, for giving me
everything I need. Thank You for
giving me the things I want
that are good for me."

It makes God happy to hear all of your prayers. But there is one prayer that God loves the most. And that is the prayer you pray when you ask Jesus to come into your heart. This is the prayer that makes God smile.

God loves you so much that He sent His Son, Jesus, to earth to save you. That's why He is called your Savior. He saves you from ever having to be separated from God.

When you receive Jesus, it means that someday you will go to heaven and live with God. Jesus said that the only way to get to heaven is by receiving Him into our hearts first. We can't find the way without Jesus.

Heaven is a wonderful place. In heaven you will never get sick and you will never be hurt. In heaven there are no bad people and nothing scary ever happens. That means you won't ever be afraid or sad. In heaven, you will be happy all the time.

God wants you to be in heaven with Him one day. That's why He sent Jesus to help you get there. But Jesus doesn't just help you get to heaven. He helps you in every way here on earth.

He helps you by being with you all of the time. He helps you by listening to you and answering your prayers. Jesus helps you by giving you everything you need. He helps you by being with you when you are sick and comforting you when you get hurt. That's why Jesus is God's greatest gift to all of us.

Jesus is the most important name in the world. Once you invite Jesus into your heart, you can call His name and He will be right there beside you.

You can't see the air, but you know it is there because you are breathing it. You can't see Jesus, but you know He is there because He has promised to be with you forever, and He never breaks His promise. Just as the air is always there keeping you alive, Jesus is always there giving you life too.

"Dear Jesus, thank You
that You will always
be with me."

When you **pray** to receive Jesus into your heart, you become one of **God's special kids.** He is your **friend forever,** and you can talk to Him whenever you want.

If something goes wrong, you can **tell Him** about it and He will help you. If you feel sad, **you can share** that with Him and He will help you **feel happy** again. And when you are having a good day, He will help you **do things for other people** that make them feel good too.

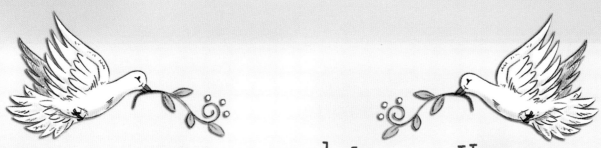

Jesus said that those who believe in Him will have their names written in a big book in heaven called the Book of Life. He said we should be very happy about that. When you receive Jesus into your heart, your name will be written in that big book too.

You get to make choices every day. You choose which toy to play with or which story to read. You choose the words you speak and many of the things you do. Receiving Jesus into your heart is also a choice you get to make. Jesus wants you to choose to receive Him. You get to decide when and where.

When you are ready to receive Jesus into your heart, you can say the prayer on the next page. You only have to say it once if you really mean it.

After you pray this prayer, write your name on the line below and put in the date. That way you will always remember when you said the prayer that makes God smile. And it will remind you that your name is written in God's big book in heaven.

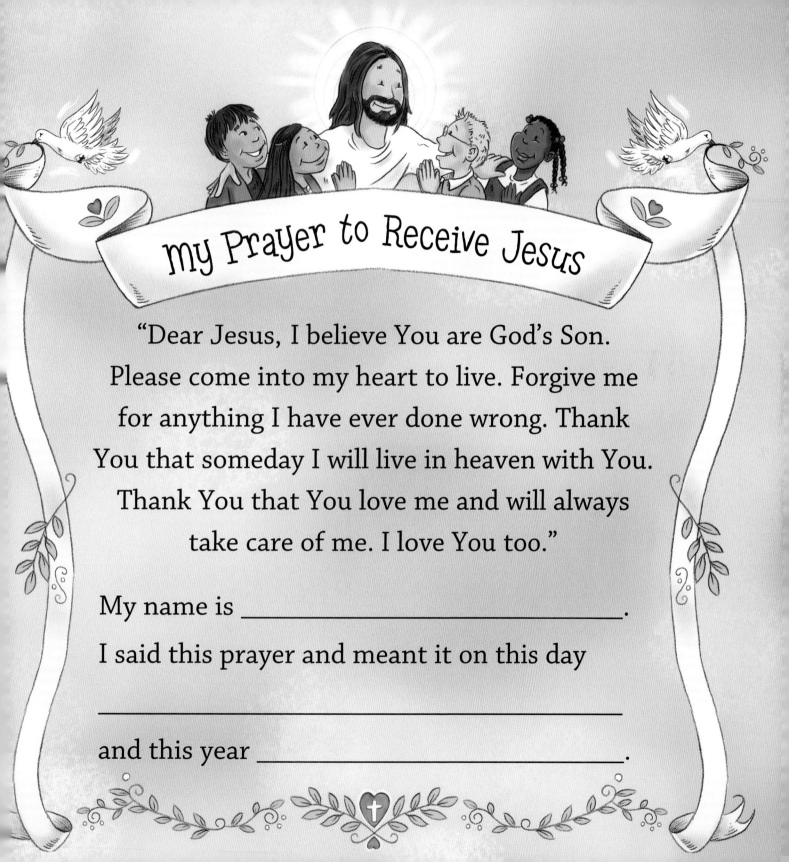

My Prayer to Receive Jesus

"Dear Jesus, I believe You are God's Son. Please come into my heart to live. Forgive me for anything I have ever done wrong. Thank You that someday I will live in heaven with You. Thank You that You love me and will always take care of me. I love You too."

My name is _____.

I said this prayer and meant it on this day

_____

and this year _____.

Once you have said this prayer, you don't ever need to say it again. You can if you want to, but you don't have to because God has heard it and Jesus has come into your heart. But there is another prayer that God loves to hear you pray, and you can say it every day if you would like to. It is the prayer on the next page, and every time you pray it, it makes God happy.

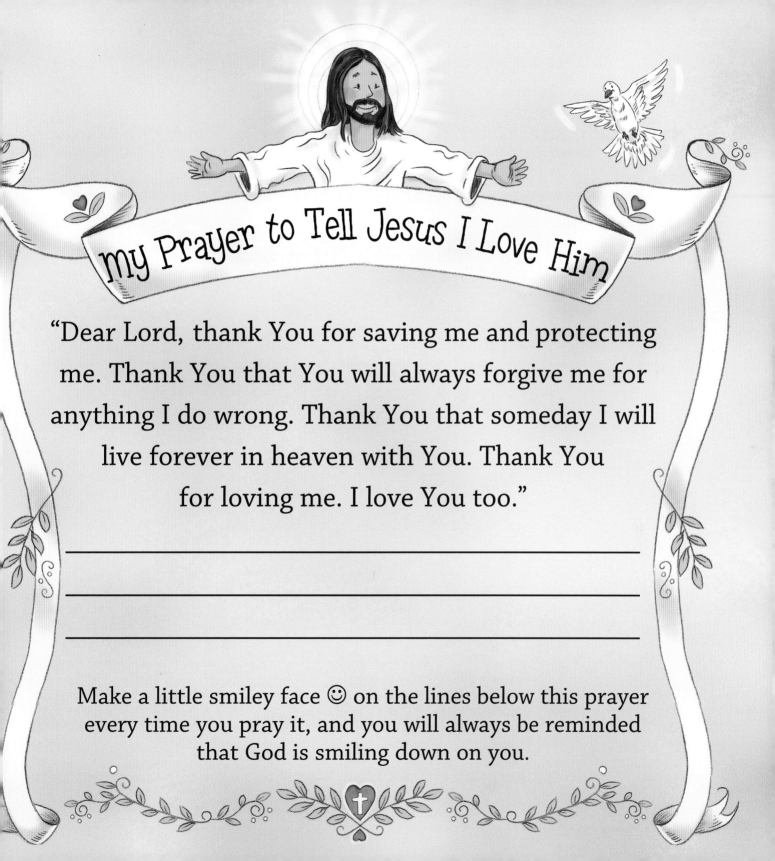

My Prayer to Tell Jesus I Love Him

"Dear Lord, thank You for saving me and protecting me. Thank You that You will always forgive me for anything I do wrong. Thank You that someday I will live forever in heaven with You. Thank You for loving me. I love You too."

_____

_____

_____

Make a little smiley face ☺ on the lines below this prayer every time you pray it, and you will always be reminded that God is smiling down on you.

The Bible says that every time someone receives Jesus as their Savior, God's angels in heaven are very happy. They are happy because God is happy. Happy people smile, and that makes others around them smile. If God and His angels are smiling, this must mean that the sun and the clouds and the flowers and birds and turtles and the rest of the animals are smiling too. And this means that the angels in heaven and all of God's creation on earth are smiling when you pray the prayer that makes God smile.

"Thank You, God,
that You are always
smiling down on me."